AF112836

This book belongs to:

_____

| Gifted by: | Date: |
|---|---|
|  |  |

If found, reward:

*a Billion dollars!*
_____

...re we beginning to commend ourselves again? Or d... ...eed, like some people, letters of recommendation to yo... ...om you? You yourselves are our letter, written on our he... ...nown and read by everyone. You show that you are a l... ...om Christ, the result of our ministry, written not with ink... ...ith the Spirit of the living God, not on tablets of stone bu... ...ablets of human hearts. Such confidence we have through C... ...efore God. Not that we are competent in ourselves to c... ...nything for ourselves, but our competence comes from G... ...e has made us competent as ministers of a new covenant— ...f the letter but of the Spirit, for the letter kills, but the S... ...ives life. Now if the ministry that brought death, which ... ...ngraved in letters on stone, came with glory, so that ... ...sraelites could not look steadily at the face of Moses beca... ...f its glory, transitory though it was, will not the ministr... ...he Spirit be even more glorious? If the ministry that brou... ...ondemnation was glorious, how much more glorious is ... ...inistry that brings righteousness! For what was glorious has... ...lory now in comparison with the surpassing glory. And if w... ...as transitory came with glory, how much greater is the gl... ...f that which lasts! Therefore, since we have such a hope, ... ...re very bold. We are not like Moses, who would put a veil o... ...is face to prevent the Israelites from seeing the end of w... ...as passing away. But their minds were made dull, for to t... ...ay the same veil remains when the old covenant is read. It ... ...ot been removed, because only in Christ is it taken away. E... ...o this day when Moses is read, a veil covers their hearts. ... ...henever anyone turns to the Lord, the veil is taken away. N... ...he Lord is the Spirit, and where the Spirit of the Lord is, th... ...s freedom. And we all, who with unveiled faces contemplate ... ...ord's glory, are being transformed into his image with ev... ...ncreasing glory, which comes from the Lord, who is the Sp...

**THE INVITATION**

**THE INVITATION**

**EXPERIENCE
GOD'S TANGIBLE
LOVE DAILY**

# JESSI GREEN

SALT PRESS

The Invitation

Copyright © 2026 by Jessi Green

All rights reserved.

Published in the United States by Salt House Press.

No part of this publication may be reproduced, distributed, or transmitted in any form or by any means, including photocopying, recording, or other electronic or mechanical methods, without the prior written permission of the publisher, except as permitted by U.S. copyright law. For permission requests, contact team@saturateglobal.com

Unless otherwise noted, all Scripture quotations are taken from the New International Version® (NIV®). Copyright © 1973, 1978, 1984, 2011 by Biblica, Inc.™ Used by permission of Zondervan. All rights reserved worldwide. For more information, visit www.zondervan.com. The "NIV" and "New International Version" are trademarks registered in the United States Patent and Trademark Office by Biblica, Inc.™

Scripture quotations marked (AMP) are taken from the Amplified® Bible, Copyright © 2015 by The Lockman Foundation. Used by permission. For more information, visit www.lockman.org.

Scripture quotations marked (ESV) are taken from The ESV® Bible (The Holy Bible, English Standard Version®), Copyright © 2001 by Crossway, a publishing ministry of Good News Publishers. Used by permission. All rights reserved.

Scripture quotations marked (NKJV) are taken from the New King James Version®. Copyright © 1982 by Thomas Nelson. Used by permission. All rights reserved.

Scripture quotations marked (NLT) are taken from the Holy Bible, New Living Translation, Copyright © 1996, 2004, 2015 by Tyndale House Foundation. Used by permission of Tyndale House Publishers, Carol Stream, Illinois 60188. All rights reserved.

Scripture quotations marked (RSV) are taken from the Revised Standard Version of the Bible, Copyright © 1946, 1952, and 1971 by the National Council of the Churches of Christ in the United States of America. Used by permission. All rights reserved worldwide.

Edited by Emily Powers White Stone Media
Cover and interior design by Gabe Schut for Each+Every
and photos and design by Victoria Panther for The Created co.

ISBN: 979-8-9944407-0-4

First Edition, 2026

I dedicate this book to my love,
Parker Green.

You have taught me how to abide in His presence when the world demands performance. You lead our family into His shelter—the place where true life is found. Thank you for teaching our family, and a generation, to pursue Jesus above all else. I love you—forever.

# Let's *begin* Our Journey

*into God's Presence*

# hi, i'm Jessi

I am here to go on this
journey with you.

# Welcome to The Invitation

I don't know what brought you to this moment, with this book in your hands, but I believe God is calling you deeper.

Maybe you're like me, and you know there is *more* available. You want to experience God's love and tangible presence every day. You want to recognize and remove the distractions that limit you from being who God has created you to be.

Or perhaps you're like my close friends . . . the women I originally wrote this book for. For my 40th birthday, we went to Tuscany, and during a late-night conversation as the sun was setting, we had enough pause to finally get honest. We yearned for more, yet felt overwhelmed. These friends love Jesus but now have kids, full-time jobs, early mornings, and a never-ending to-do list. When they have any spare time (is that even a thing?), they feel the pull to be more productive, to be present with their family—and then God gets the breadcrumbs. Maybe you're also navigating disappointments, delayed dreams, and heartache, yet longing to awaken first love for Jesus again.

Maybe there's another reason, and you can't quite find the words yet, but your prayer has become a quiet whisper: "I want to want You, Jesus."

One of my favorite Bible verses is:

"For God says, 'At just the right time, I heard you. On the day of salvation, I helped you.' Indeed, the 'right time' is now. Today is the day of salvation."[1]

---

[1] 2 Corinthians 6:2 NLT

"For God says, 'At just the right time, I heard you. On the day of salvation, I helped you.' Indeed, the 'right time' is now. Today is the day of salvation."

— *2 Corinthians 6:2 NLT*

Today, God is drawing you deeper into His love, teaching you how to abide in His presence . . . now and tomorrow, too.

I remember when God's invitation to go deeper arrived. I had been praying during a Bible study to "feel more of His love" and to be "filled with His power," but when His invitation came, I hesitated, afraid to loosen my grip on comfort and risk my reputation. I was being invited to encounter the very love I longed for, yet instead of receiving it, I tried to protect myself.

I didn't know that tears are often the wax seal on the invitation God sends—His call to step into His presence in both the monumental and the mundane.

When was the last time you cried in His presence? I mean, really cried. Snot and all.

In His presence is peace, silencing the low hum of anxiety. Joy that rises beyond human control or explanation. Love that heals the pain of the past, and power that lifts the crippled out of their wheelchairs.

In His Presence is Jesus.

I AM SET FREE
SET FREE

SET FREE
FREE
FREE

PLEASE GOD!

SHE IS BOTH MUSE AND CREATOR
AND YOU LOVE THE WAY SHE BLURS THE LINE
BETWEEN ART AND LIFE.

Not a goosebump, but the Lord Himself is with you.

This is the love and power we have access to—daily.

Yet, most of the time, I do what many of us do:
I close the envelope and return it to the Sender.

Maybe you're like me. You want to experience more of God, but life feels overwhelming.

✓ Busy
 ✓ Crowded
  ✓ Dis tract ed

And when the sacred moments interrupt our hurried days, we ignore them.

Will you give me fourteen days to walk you through a process to truly encounter God's tangible love and power, to discover what He's called you to do, and to overcome the fear of man and the need to control?

I asked my friends this same question and they texted back, "Heck, yes! I need exactly that right now."

God led the five of us deeper.
And everything changed.

People on the street began getting saved, and we saw more people physically healed in our church services. Miracles and moments where we could feel His love invading our days became more and more normal. Our group text exploded with, "This is crazy!"

Maybe below, you simply need to scribble a "Heck, yes!" or "Please, God!"—your way of agreeing to whatever Jesus desires to do.

And just because life is messy, and sometimes we need to experience something real and tangible to step into our breakthrough, the back of this book is filled with pages you can rip out and put in your wallet, give to a friend, cut out and glue into your journal, or hand to a stranger.

## Day 1
# Burn the Candle

Some call it high cortisol.
Overstimulation.
There's a longing for God's presence, but it's buried beneath laundry, the latest scandal on social media, or an endless pile of Amazon returns.

I want to remember the feeling of God's tangible love and power I experienced on the beaches of California in the summer of 2020. I preached the Gospel through a $60 megaphone, and waves of people ran into the ocean to repent and be baptized. I witnessed miracles with my own eyes as the presence of God burned through me.

## Los Angeles Times
### In Huntington Beach, A Church Revival at the Ocean's Edge

The *LA Times* reported "Revival Hits the Beaches of California."

Life looks a little bit different now.

"Mom! We're out of Chick-fil-A sauce!" my five-year-old, Summer, screamed.

It felt less like a normal Tuesday and more like a mental and spiritual ambush. My four children shouted down the halls like sirens while my Instagram feed showed thin, tanned, filtered moms on gingham blankets, eating watermelon in a perfectly manicured garden. I set my phone down and hurried to plate overcooked smash-burgers to my screaming (and very passionate) children.

## Day 1: Burn the Candle

We gathered around the table with French fries, grilled onions, and at least six sauces per person. We're a sauce family. My husband, Parker, leaned in behind me for a kiss—a sweet, ordinary gesture . . . and I flinched.

His face dropped.

I don't want to be *that* kind of woman. My soul was tired, and honestly, I felt forgotten in the world of revival, like Cinderella when it came to my calling.

After the kids' bedtime routine, I caught up on emails and cornered Parker in the kitchen about a staff situation in our new church. He has a strict "no work after 5:00 p.m." policy. I break it almost daily.

"I'm not working," I quickly reply. "I just need to process my feelings."

I fall into bed at the end of the day and set four alarms: 5:00, 5:15, 6:00, and 6:30 a.m.

The truth?

I long for God's presence. I bet you do, too.

I want to truly experience His love overflowing in me—you know, the whole river of living water. Yet, I feel stuck, and the worst part is I'm supposed to be a professional at this.

I've read *The Ruthless Elimination of Hurry*.[2]

*Twice.*

But Sunday mornings still find me curling my hair while the kids wait in the car. I keep my makeup bag in the glove box. Mascara gets applied as we pass the Starbucks and turn down the 210 Highway in Hampstead.

Sometimes I fantasize about being a missionary somewhere remote and gritty. Instead, I'm buying organic feta for $8.00 at Whole Foods and wondering why the math ain't mathin' on my recent Amex statement.

I want to live in the *fullness* of what God planned for me before I was born. I want to experience the real, tangible

---

[2] Comer, John Mark. *The Ruthless Elimination of Hurry*. Colorado Springs, CO: WaterBrook, 2019.

## Day 1: Burn the Candle

love and power of God every single day—not just preach revival but live it . . . on a Tuesday.

And that brings us to the candle.

Every Friday at 5 a.m., around twenty men show up in our garage to lift weights with Parker. They cold-plunge and pray together.

I sipped my macadamia milk latte, curled under a blanket on our big white couch with stained cushions, listening as the house shakes with every dumbbell dropped in the garage. On the coffee table sat a $500 Le Labo candle that smelled amazing. (I completely understand how ridiculous it is to own a $500 candle—trust me. It was a gift from my friend Kendall when my book *Wildfires*[3] launched. Kendall is great at celebrating her friends' wins.)

I reached for a lighter.
Paused.
*Special occasions only,* I thought.

---

[3] Green, Jessi. 2021. *Wildfires: Revolt Against Apathy and Ignite Your World with God's Power.* Colorado Springs: Destiny Image Incorporated.

*If I burn it now, it'll be gone.*

Then the whisper:
"Jessi, burn the candle."
So, I did—but hesitantly.

The flickering flame drew me in as the scent of the candle filled the room. It was a small, holy declaration: *I refuse to believe that beauty must be earned, that joy must wait, that the presence of God is reserved for some future version of myself.*

What if the most miraculous moments aren't found at conferences or in crowded revival tents? What if they're found here—in this quiet space—when everyone is asleep, and you slowly read the Word as it searches you?

I quietly jotted in my journal, *Is spiritual formation just for the boys?*

# my favorite candles

BUCK MASON

LE LABO SANTAL

CAPRI BLUE FIR AND FIREWOOD

FEU DE BOIS

It's time to take out your journal and *Light a candle*

slowly write:

"'In the time of My favor I heard you, and in the day of salvation I helped you.' I tell you, now is the time of God's favor, now is the day of salvation."
— 2 Corinthians 6:2

DO YOU BELIEVE THAT *now* IS THE TIME OF GOD'S FAVOR?

WHAT ARE YOU THANKFUL TO BE SAVED *from*?

WHAT IS DISTRACTING YOU FROM GOD'S PRESENCE *now*?

## REMEMBER SURRENDER

## Remember Surrender

Don't move on to the next day until you feel settled into this rhythm. Burn a candle next to your bed and take five minutes to pause. Ask the Holy Spirit to reveal the presence of Jesus and speak to you. Record *anything* you hear, see, think, or imagine.

# Day 2
# Access to God

The shower is a magic portal into the throne room of Almighty God.

Early each morning, around 6:00 a.m., before my children demand pancakes sprinkled with cinnamon sugar, I turn the unlacquered brass knob all the way to the left and wait for steam to billow over the glass door. I wish I was one of those people who neatly folds their clothes on the bathroom counter, but alas, mine usually end up in a messy pile—one that will likely remain there until my kind husband picks them up along with his wet bathing suit from his post-workout cold plunge.

As I step into the shower, I turn the knob slightly to the right to cool the temperature from scalding to merely very warm. Parker insists my showers are too hot, and I'll admit my back is usually red when I step out—but honestly, who can tolerate a cold shower? I once read a book by Victoria Beckham in which she said she took cold showers to improve her hair and skin. I tried it for a few days. It wasn't worth it. Just go online and order some collagen—problem solved.

As my head finds its way under the manufactured rain drops, there it is.
No distractions.
The to-do list can't be written.
The phone can't be answered.

✯ It is here that I truly hear from God. ✯

As I begin rinsing the soapy purple suds of brass-toning shampoo from my blonde locks, my thoughts untangle and grow uncluttered. The Bible verses I read that morning suddenly orchestrate themselves into meaning for my life.

I close my eyes tightly and see a vision—a low country boil with crab and corn spread across newspapers on a long wooden table. Baptisms. Country line dancing. Hayrides with a banjo strumming in the background as people kick off their cowboy boots and decide to repent and follow Jesus.

No one gets saved at a low country boil—well, not yet…

I finish rinsing out the shampoo and see another movie play before my eyes: a staircase lined with thick long candles, flowing oversized satin bows, cupcakes with candied pearls delicately placed on top, and—dare I say—champagne. A secret society of women gathering in an old penthouse apartment in Manhattan, dressed in glittering gowns, conspiring and laughing as they pray for cultural transformation to restore biblical femininity.

Finally stepping out of the shower, I wrap myself in the fluffiest oversized white towel you can imagine (that I somehow found at Target). Droplets of warm water still trail down my neck from my soaked hair as I curl up in bed.

I scramble around the room to find a lighter (my kids steal all of mine to start fires in the backyard), finally ignite a flame, and light a candle that smells like s'mores. Then I open to Exodus in my leather study Bible and begin to read the following passage:

> You shall make an altar on which to burn incense; you shall make it of acacia wood. A cubit shall be its length, and a cubit its breadth. It shall be square, and two cubits shall be its height. Its horns shall be of one piece with it. You shall overlay it with pure gold, its top and its sides all around and its horns. And you shall make a molding of gold around it. And you shall make two golden rings for it. Under its molding, on two opposite sides of it, you shall make them, and they shall be holders for poles with which to carry it. You shall make the poles of acacia wood and overlay them with gold. And you shall put it in front of the veil that is above the ark of the testimony, in front of the mercy seat that is above the testimony, where I will meet with you.[4]

---

[4]   Exodus 30:1-6 ESV

## Day 2: Access to God

Acacia wood, cubits, gold rings, incense—open up Exodus and fall into the story. Even the timing of the offerings was important to the Lord. As I slowly read through each elaborate detail, not pretending to understand it all, but inviting the Holy Spirit to teach me, I recognize the beautiful invitation God extended to His people.

God is not random or unintentional.
With intentionality and beauty, He granted us the ability to access His Presence—an invitation to pray, commune, and meet with the Creator of the universe.

The One who imagined the stars and spoke life into being desires a meeting with us.

The design, materials, and instructions for Israel to attend this divine gathering were so specific, so thoughtfully considered. In the Old Testament, upon the mercy seat within the tabernacle, God declared to His people, "There will I meet with you." This passage describes the altar of incense placed in the Holy Place—right outside the Most Holy Place.

It's almost hard to imagine, in our age of large projection screens and big stages, ninety-second TikTok sermons, and endless Bible reading plans we start but rarely finish, that ministers were once consecrated—set apart solely to offer prayer to God on behalf of themselves and His people. They could meet with God, but only when He chose to meet with them, and in the manner He prescribed.

Today, do we even know how to meet with God now that we have full access?

**It's time to take out your journal, light a candle, and slowly answer this question:**

Pause. Breathe.
What is God whispering to your heart right now?

Sit in stillness for ten minutes, and let His words find you—then, write what you hear.

Ask the Holy Spirit, where do I hear your voice the most clearly?

Day 2: Access to God

It's time to take out your journal and

*Light a candle*

slowly answer this question:

WHAT IS GOD WHISPERING TO
YOUR HEART RIGHT NOW?

pause. breathe.

Sit in stillness for ten minutes, and let His
words find you -- then write what you hear.

ASK THE HOLY SPIRIT,
WHERE DO I HEAR YOUR VOICE

THE *most* CLEARLY?

## Remember Surrender:

One of my favorite books of all time is by A.W. Tozer, *The Pursuit of God*. In the book, Tozer invites readers to tune into God's voice. He writes:

> The Voice of God is a friendly Voice. No one need fear to listen to it unless he has already made up his mind to resist it . . . Whoever will listen will hear the speaking heaven. This is definitely not the hour when men take kindly to an exhortation to listen, for listening is not a part of popular religion today. We are at the opposite end of the pole from there. Religion has accepted the monstrous heresy that noise, size, activity, and bluster make a man dear to God. But we may take heart. To a people caught in the tempest of the last great conflict God says, 'Be still, and know that I am God' (Psalm 46:10), and still He says it, as if He means to tell us that our strength and safety lie not in noise but in silence.[5]

---

[5] Tozer, A. W. *The Pursuit of God: The Human Thirst for the Divine*. Harrisburg, PA: Christian Publications, 1948, 75.

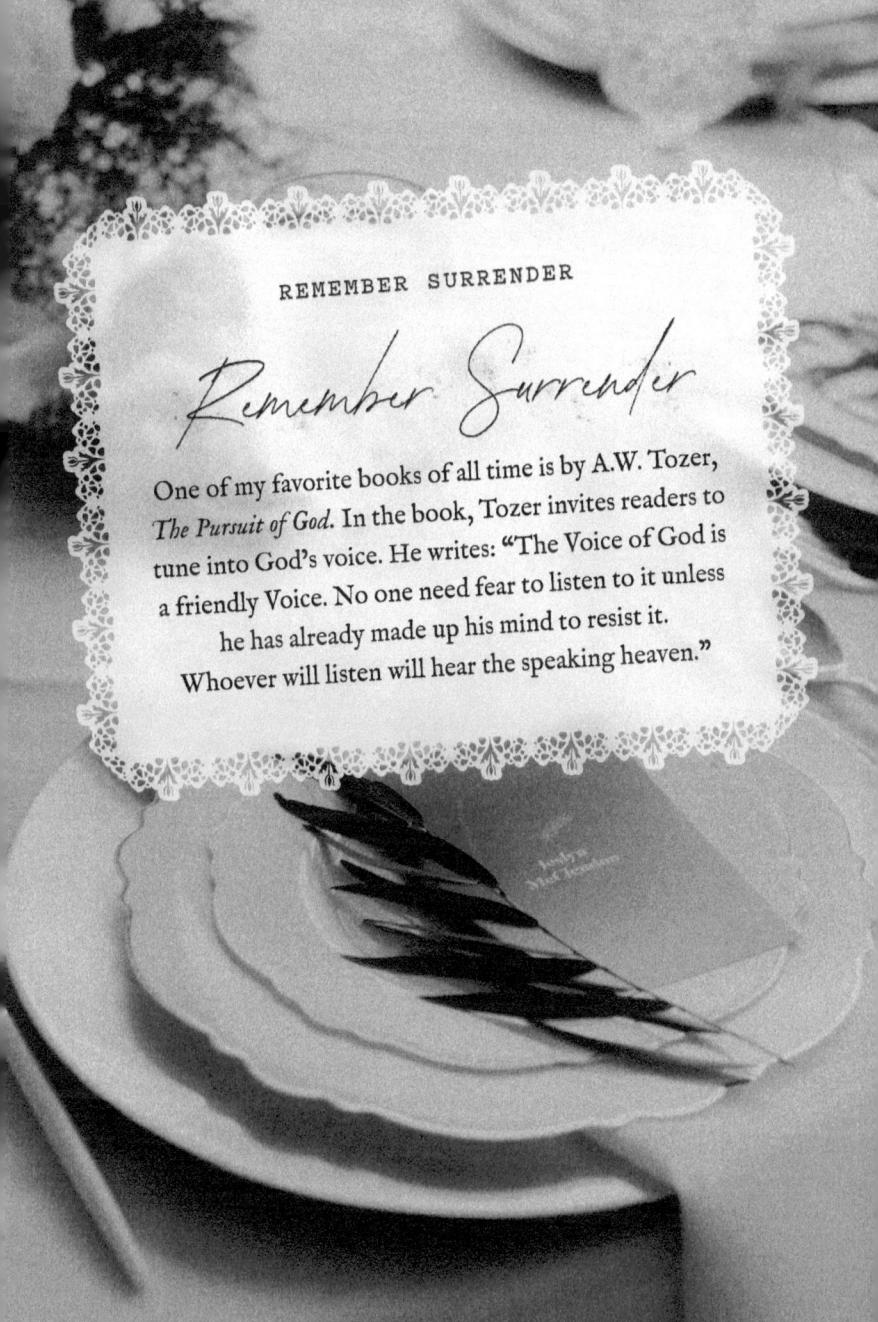

## REMEMBER SURRENDER

*Remember Surrender*

One of my favorite books of all time is by A.W. Tozer, *The Pursuit of God*. In the book, Tozer invites readers to tune into God's voice. He writes: "The Voice of God is a friendly Voice. No one need fear to listen to it unless he has already made up his mind to resist it. Whoever will listen will hear the speaking heaven."

# Day 3
# In His Shelter

There's a fire that burns around you and a fire that burns within you.

The wildfire of God consumes everything that's dead, unfruitful, and unholy. But inside that blaze, there's a secret place—a quiet center of safety and intimacy, like the eye of a hurricane.

Psalm 91 calls it *the shadow of the Almighty.* This has become a life Scripture for me. Maybe you need to tear that page out of your Bible (I conveniently put one in the back of this book if you don't want to rip apart your Bible) and keep it in your pocket.

The Jewish people carry God's words close to their bodies. They put a written passage of Scripture in a small leather box and wear it on their arm or forehead. We need to wear the Word. When I feel far from God, I turn to Psalm 91, and over the last five years of leading revival, I have had to learn how to put it on.

I have to reread it often, because in the busyness of life, I forget. Sometimes, I feel so overwhelmed I just want to hide or run away. I will cry out in my shower, "Hide me in You, God!" I will grab my son Ethan in the kitchen and wrap my arms around him, putting my weight on his body so he can really feel me covering him. I tell Ethan, "This is what it feels like—hiding in the shelter of God, where He covers you, where nothing can come against you."

God's love for you is described as a consuming fire. It's the kind of fire that burns away the counterfeit and reveals the gold within you. When you feel like you're at the end of yourself, you are nearer to the fire than you can imagine! No masks or pain from your past or idol that tries to exalt itself in your heart can survive the flame.

## Day 3: In His Shelter

Psalm 91 is the invitation to dwell in His Presence. Please hear me, there is so much more for you than a visitation every Sunday.

**What three things stick out to you in this chapter?**

1.

2.

3.

**It's time to take out your journal, light a candle, and write this slowly:**

The psalmist says, "He will cover you with His feathers, and under His wings you will find refuge."[6]

It's the mystery of divine protection, habitation in God, and purification all at once. You can burn with holy fire and still be hidden under His wings. You can feel the intensity of His call and still rest in His covering.

This is what it means to live out revival and rest—to be a burning one who still abides. This is my deepest desire, my daily prayer.

---

[6] Psalm 91:4

## Day 3: In His Shelter

It's time to take out your journal and *Light a candle*

slowly write:

"Whoever dwells in the shelter of the Most High
    will rest in the shadow of the Almighty.
I will say of the Lord,
    "He is my refuge and my fortress,
    my God, in whom I trust."

Surely he will save you
    from the fowler's snare
    and from the deadly pestilence.
He will cover you with his feathers,
    and under his wings you will find refuge;
    his faithfulness will be your shield and
    rampart.
You will not fear the terror of night,
    nor the arrow that flies by day,
    nor the pestilence that stalks in the darkness,
    nor the plague that destroys at midday.

THE INVITATION

A thousand may fall at your side,
    ten thousand at your right hand,
    but it will not come near you.
You will only observe with your eyes
    and see the punishment of the wicked.

If you say, "The Lord is my refuge,"
    and you make the Most High your dwelling,
    no harm will overtake you,
    no disaster will come near your tent.
For he will command his angels concerning you
    to guard you in all your ways;
    they will lift you up in their hands,
    so that you will not strike your foot
    against a stone.
You will tread on the lion and the cobra; you
    will trample the great lion and the serpent.

"Because he loves me," says the Lord,
    "I will rescue him;
    I will protect him, for he acknowledges
    my name.
He will call on me, and I will answer him;
    I will be with him in trouble,
    I will deliver him and honor him.
With long life I will satisfy him and show him
    my salvation."[6]

---

6    Psalm 91:1-16

REMEMBER SURRENDER

*Remember Surrender*

Lord, I choose to dwell in Your presence and rest. Father, draw me into Your secret place. Help me to experience more of Your love and presence. Cover me under the shadow of Your wings.

**Remember Surrender:**

As the candle flame rises, whisper this:

"Lord, I choose to dwell in Your presence and rest."

Sit in silence for five minutes.
Let His presence be the flame,
and your heart the wick.

Then pray with me softly:

Father, draw me into Your secret place.
Help me to experience more of Your love and presence.
Cover me under the shadow of Your wings.

Let my life burn for You.
Protect my heart and my mind from every attack of the enemy.
Holy Spirit, empower me to make the Lord my dwelling place. I don't want to leave your presence.

What needs to be changed in my life to make you my priority?

Amen.

# Day 4
# The Lie of Later

When life slows down . . . when the kids grow up . . . *when* I finally feel certain of what God wants me to do, *then* I'll step fully into my calling and identity in Christ.

"Later" is when I'll spend time in God's presence.

And in the meantime?
We keep scrolling.

We order one more $40 water bottle—just another thing to organize.

We become increasingly strategic with our time and better managers of our budget, but the peace Christ offers us feels more like a good idea than a reality.

We have a real problem.

One in three women say they constantly feel rushed, even during their downtime.[7]

Maybe you're like me—you love God, but you feel stuck. Stuck in doubt about who you are and whether you're truly called by God. Stuck in fear of others' opinions, fear of the future. Stuck in the endless cycle of indecision. Stuck in "what could have been."

That was me.

I knew how to say "yes" with my lips but lived most days managing risk, controlling outcomes, and delaying obedience.

*But faith doesn't work like that.*

According to a Barna study, only 21% of Christian women say they feel free—truly surrendered to God's will in

---

7   Pew Research Center. *How Americans View Time, Money, Work, and Community*. Washington, D.C.: Pew Research Center, 2022. https://www.pewresearch.org/social-trends/2022/10/05/how-americans-view-time-money-work-and-community/

## Day 4: The Lie of Later

their daily life. The majority report feeling "pressured to hold it all together."[8]

Radical obedience often comes before radical clarity. And the longer we wait for every detail to make sense, the more we trade the fire of God for the illusion of control.

There's a story in Scripture that immediately silences the loud voice in my head that says, "Now isn't the right time." It's the story of the woman who brought an alabaster jar of perfume to Jesus in a crowded room of men. She didn't really belong there; she wasn't qualified—she was simply obsessed with Jesus.

She broke it open and poured it out on His feet.
All of it.
No backup plan.

She gave Him everything, in front of everyone.
Extravagant love disrupted the room, but she didn't care what they thought.

---

[8] Barna Group. *The State of Women in the Church.* Ventura, CA: Barna Group, 2021. https://www.barna.com/research/state-of-women-in-the-church/

While some of my friends relate to Esther or Deborah, I cry out to God to make me like Mary. I want to recognize that Jesus is with me. Every day, I want to pour out my life to him, I want to give it all—100%—holding nothing back.

"'Why this waste?' they asked. 'This perfume could have been sold at a high price and the money given to the poor.'"[9]

I often feel guilty enjoying the presence of God—anyone else? Like maybe I need to answer a few hundred more emails, build another spreadsheet, organize another event, feed my children a perfectly cooked organic dinner, and prove to God that I belong in the room.

But Jesus said something to the onlookers:

"She has done a beautiful thing to me . . . wherever this gospel is preached throughout the world, what she has done will also be told, in memory of her."[10]

---

9    Matthew 26:8-9
10   Matthew 26:10, 13

## Day 4: The Lie of Later

She saw that Jesus was with her, and she responded.

I used to think I'd rest more once everything was under control. But control is just anxiety in a prettier outfit. Every time I delay obedience, I trade wonder for worry. I tell God, *When this happens, then I'll give You everything.*

You guys, sometimes life is messy. You accidentally hit snooze and scramble to get out the door. You receive a surprise medical diagnosis, and joy feels a million miles away. Most days don't look perfect—they look like finding your Bible buried beneath the laundry at the foot of your bed.

You just need to pour out what you have *now*.

Maybe the most radical act of faith in this generation isn't doing more for God . . . it's putting down the phone, silencing the noise, and letting love interrupt you again. My husband, Parker, often reminds me, "Following Jesus is less about adding things to your life and more about removing whatever distracts you from Him."

**It's time to take out your journal, light a candle, and slowly write:**

The lie says: "You'll find peace once life slows down."
The truth says: "Peace is a Person sitting in your living room."
Where are you too busy? Still striving?

## Day 4: The Lie of Later

It's time to take out your journal and

*Light a candle*

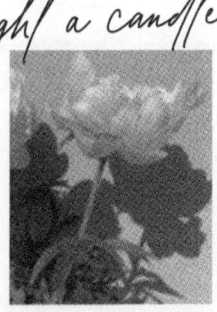

slowly write:

THE LIE SAYS:
"You'll find peace once life slows down."

THE TRUTH SAYS:
"Peace is a Person sitting in your living room."

WHERE ARE YOU *too busy*?
STILL STRIVING?

### Step one — write your "when/then" lie.

Write down one statement that starts with: When _____ happens, then I'll really follow God.

*For example: When I have more time, then I'll start journaling before I go to bed. When I'm certain of the next step, then I'll start training for it. When I feel ready to confront the truth, then I'll have that hard conversation. When my kids are all in school, then I'll prioritize time to share the Gospel with people on the street.*

### Step two — cross out the lie.

Physically draw a bold line through the lie and write beneath it: Now! I choose to follow Jesus now.

### Step three — respond in the moment.

Take one small act of extravagant love toward God today: a moment of worship, generosity, surrender, or obedience that is inconvenient.

### Step four — behold what happens.

Notice the peace that rushes in when you stop delaying surrender.

*Tear the page out! Take it with you and live this truth.*

# my when/then lie

When:
..................................................................................................

Then:
..................................................................................................

When:
..................................................................................................

Then:
..................................................................................................

step two - copy the statement

*Now! I choose to follow Jesus now.*

↓

BEHOLD WHAT HAPPENS.

Notice the peace that rushes in when you
stop delaying surrender.

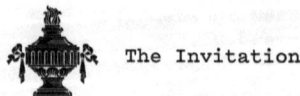 The Invitation

 JESSI GREEN
—— WITH LOVE, ALWAYS

*Day 5*

# Do Not Resist the Father's Love

Two years ago, I was at a fancy restaurant in Charlotte. I had ordered a medium-well steak with a side of broccolini. I don't normally order steak, but we were at one of the best steakhouses in the city, so I figured it was worth trying.

Gathered around the table were some of our favorite speakers and ministry leaders—authors, preachers, and YouTube sensations with millions of followers. A well-known Christian studio with international reach had invited Parker and I to host our own show. We would film twelve episodes in just two days (that is a lot of talking—even for me) and have the privilege of asking these leaders our burning questions about following Jesus, revival, the prophetic, and more. I was so excited, but also so nervous. I felt completely unqualified to be in the room. How did I get here?

As we waited for our entrées to arrive, the table buzzed with conversation—about the next day's filming schedule, the upcoming election, recent ministry adventures, and even which airline was the best. Across from me sat Eddie and Janet Piorek.

Eddie Piorek was one of the primary disciples of John Wimber, the founder and leader of the Vineyard movement and a central figure in the Jesus People movement in Southern California.

Eddie is a laid-back surfer who lives in sunny San Clemente. He had pastored one of the Vineyard churches in Orange County and helped lead the Toronto Blessing in the early '90s. In 2020, as Parker and I were thrust into revival on the California coast during the pandemic, we talked with John and Carol Arnott, the pastors of the outpouring in Toronto. They suggested Parker connect with Eddie.

## Day 5: Do Not Resist the Father's Love

Parker drove down to San Clemente to meet with him. I did not attend but stayed home with our three children. Parker returned from that meeting later that evening . . . different.

Honestly, I can't really explain *how* he was different, but peace had moved in and refused to leave. He felt—settled.

Sometimes I feel like an investigative reporter after Parker has met with someone.
"So, what did you guys talk about?" I asked.
"We didn't, really."
"You didn't really what?" I pressed.
"Talk."
"So, what did you do?"
"We sat there and looked at each other."

I was bewildered. I could never imagine—in a million years—going to a stranger's house and simply sitting in silence across from them.

Parker added, "We did pray together, and I cried. I wasn't expecting that."
I didn't press any further.

Parker doesn't really cry.

Over the next few months, I witnessed a transformation in Parker. The fear of living paycheck to paycheck dissipated. The frenetic energy to grow the church faster and larger ceased. Parker was more present. I'd be washing the dishes and look out the kitchen window to see him sitting on the grass, talking on the phone with Eddie. Parker never had what people call "a spiritual father." I thought, *Maybe this is what that looks like.*

Now at this dinner in Charlotte, we sat across from the man who had seemingly transformed my husband. I had so many questions, but I didn't know where to begin. I felt the weight of responsibility to host all the guests we had invited onto our show. And if I'm honest, I wanted to impress them, but I felt strangely insecure. It felt like ninth-grade Jessi, sitting at a cafeteria lunch table—not popular, mostly just existing, and trying not to draw attention to herself.

As the waitress placed my steak in front of me, I sliced into the searing meat and spread some béarnaise across the top. I asked Janet, Eddie's wife, if she liked to travel.

## Day 5: Do Not Resist the Father's Love

I didn't really care if she liked to travel; I just didn't know what else to talk about. As she answered, her voice blended in with the background noise.

Heat began to creep up my neck, and I couldn't swallow. I started to weep—excessively—into my steak. Blinded by salty tears, I scrambled to find the napkin on my lap and wipe my face, careful not to smear my mascara or draw too much attention to myself.

As my eyes refocused, I noticed Eddie's eyes locked on me—laser-focused.
He leaned in.
"I am so sorry; I don't know what is wrong with me," I muttered, grabbing Parker's leg, desperate for him to rescue me from further embarrassment.

Eddie leaned toward me even further, and with complete resolve, spoke words that would forever change my life: "Do not resist the Father's love."

This couldn't be happening.
Not now.
Not in front of all these people.

A famous preacher sitting to my left, whom I very much wanted to impress, turned toward me and asked, "Are you okay?"

"Yes, I'm good. I'm so sorry; I don't know what's happening."

My best friend Vic mouthed to me from across the table, "What in the world is going on?"
I shrugged.
I whispered to Parker, "I have to go to the bathroom."
Parker stared into my eyes and said, "That's just what Eddie does."

I was being invited to experience the love of God—the very thing I yearned for—and it embarrassed me. I feared it might damage my reputation, even among other ministers. How strange is this ministry world we live in?

I didn't yet know that tears are the wax seal on the invitation God extends, calling us into His presence daily. They interrupt us in our car, when our favorite song comes on in the nail salon, or as a rainbow appears after a rained-out event.

## Day 5: Do Not Resist the Father's Love

Yet, in that moment, I did what many of us do.

I wiped my tears and moved on.

Over the last five years, I have been on a messy and costly journey, learning how *not* to do that. I have attended some of the largest Christian gatherings in the world and sat with some of the most prominent Christian leaders. And I can tell you one thing I have learned along the way:

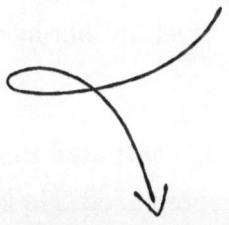

You cannot manufacture the presence of God; however, you can recognize it and collect those moments of love to sustain you.

I have watched firsthand as countless ministers manufacture energy to create excitement and gather millions of followers. With brilliant marketing and the right speaker lineup, you can hype a crowd and fill entire stadiums. Yet a month later, no one is talking about it. It hasn't marked anyone for eternity. It is forgotten.

We put our heads down and return to busyness—distracted, scrolling, arguing. We register for the next event that promises to "level up" our lives, and we are still left . . . wanting.

Over one meal, Eddie demonstrated something I had never seen before or experienced. He knew Jesus so intimately that, without a word, he could ruin a steak dinner and alter the course of my life—my focus and my pursuits. An invitation to abide was extended to me that evening, and since then, I have been reorienting my life to learn how to live it out by faith.

## Day 5: Do Not Resist the Father's Love

*Light a candle*
and pray with me:

Father God,
I want to be with You.

I repent for every
moment I've resisted
Your nearness
because it felt
inconvenient
or uncomfortable.

Teach me to recognize
Your presence
in ordinary places:
at dinners, on drives,
and while dishwashing.

Make me tender to
Your love,
aware of your whispers
through the day,
overflowing with your
mercy.

## Remember Surrender:

"And I will ask the Father, and He will give you another Advocate, who will never leave you. He is the Holy Spirit, who leads into all truth. The world cannot receive Him, because it isn't looking for Him and doesn't recognize Him. But you know Him, because He lives with you now and later will be in you.

No, I will not abandon you as orphans—I will come to you. Soon the world will no longer see Me, but you will see Me. Since I live, you also will live. When I am raised to life again, you will know that I am in My Father, and you are in Me, and I am in you.

Those who accept My commandments and obey them are the ones who love Me. And because they love Me, My Father will love them. And I will love them and reveal Myself to each of them."

## REMEMBER SURRENDER

### Remember Surrender

"No, I will not abandon you as orphans—I will come to you. Soon the world will no longer see Me, but you will see Me. Since I live, you also will live. When I am raised to life again, you will know that I am in My Father, and you are in Me, and I am in you."

Judas (not Judas Iscariot, but the other disciple with that name) said to Him, "Lord, why are You going to reveal Yourself only to us and not to the world at large?"

Jesus replied, "All who love Me will do what I say. My Father will love them, and We will come and make Our home with each of them."[11]

---

[11] John 14:16-23 NLT

# Day 6
# Turn to the Lord

In this age of cultural Christianity—full of ritual but lacking transformation—many believers, especially women, find themselves exhausted and disconnected from the life Jesus promised. We save the nice things in our homes for when guests come over and the house is clean. Maybe you are like me, and some mornings you glance at your Bible but reach for your phone. You whisper a "Help me, Jesus!" prayer while going to the bathroom or taking a quick shower.

You love Jesus. You do.
But somewhere along the way, you've lost the romance. The fire.

The wild adventure of following Jesus.
And now you're tired.
Not just physically—
*Your soul is flipping tired.*

So, you book a massage, sign up for a Pilates class, order another matcha, and plan a family vacation—anything to distract you from the fact that daily life isn't working. I know things are really bad when I find myself clicking "Buy Now" on Amazon from an influencer's storefront—something else I don't need (and sometimes don't even want). I call it "when I feel shoppy." *Shoppy* equals spiritual depression for me. It's the engine light revealing the condition of my soul.

My favorite Bible verse of all time is this:

> Therefore, since we have such a hope, we are very bold. We are not like Moses, who would put a veil over his face to prevent the Israelites from seeing the end of what was passing away. But their minds were made dull, for to this day the same veil remains when the old covenant is read.

## Day 6: Turn to the Lord

It has not been removed, because only in Christ is it taken away. Even to this day when Moses is read, a veil covers their hearts. ***But whenever anyone turns to the Lord, the veil is taken away.*** Now the Lord is the Spirit, and where the Spirit of the Lord is, there is freedom. And we all, who with unveiled faces contemplate the Lord's glory, are being transformed into his image with ever-increasing glory, which comes from the Lord, who is the Spirit.[12]

I spent five years meditating on that one verse: *"Whenever anyone turns to the Lord, the veil is taken away."* In college, I majored in poetry, and I'll admit that for years I read this as figurative language—beautifully written, but not an actual reality. Could it really be possible? One turn to the Lord, and the veil—every hindrance, every wall—is taken away?

We say we're waiting on God. Often, we're really waiting for the perfect, convenient time to follow Jesus. We save

---

[12] 2 Corinthians 3:12-18

the candle, the dress, the dream for someday. We're thankful to be forgiven of our sins. We try not to cuss. We show up to church—and yet we're missing the beauty of now.

One turn. One moment of focused attention. And there God is.

"Whenever" means any time, in any place—you can enter in.

"Anyone" means you and me, our neighbors, our family, and even our enemies.

Turning to the Lord is another way of saying repentance. When we repent, we invite the Holy Spirit to reveal where we have turned away from God, and He empowers us to return to Him. This is a daily gift—and one I find myself needing often.

## Day 6: Turn to the Lord

It's time to take out your journal and

*Light a candle*

slowly answer:

**WHAT LIES ARE YOU BELIEVING THAT ARE HOLDING YOU BACK FROM EXPERIENCING HIS TANGIBLE LOVE AND PRESENCE TODAY?**

What roadblocks are frustrating you as you try to press in *deeper*?

What are you saving for later that God wants you to use now?

Are there any ways you are relying on the world for comfort instead of placing your trust *in Christ*?

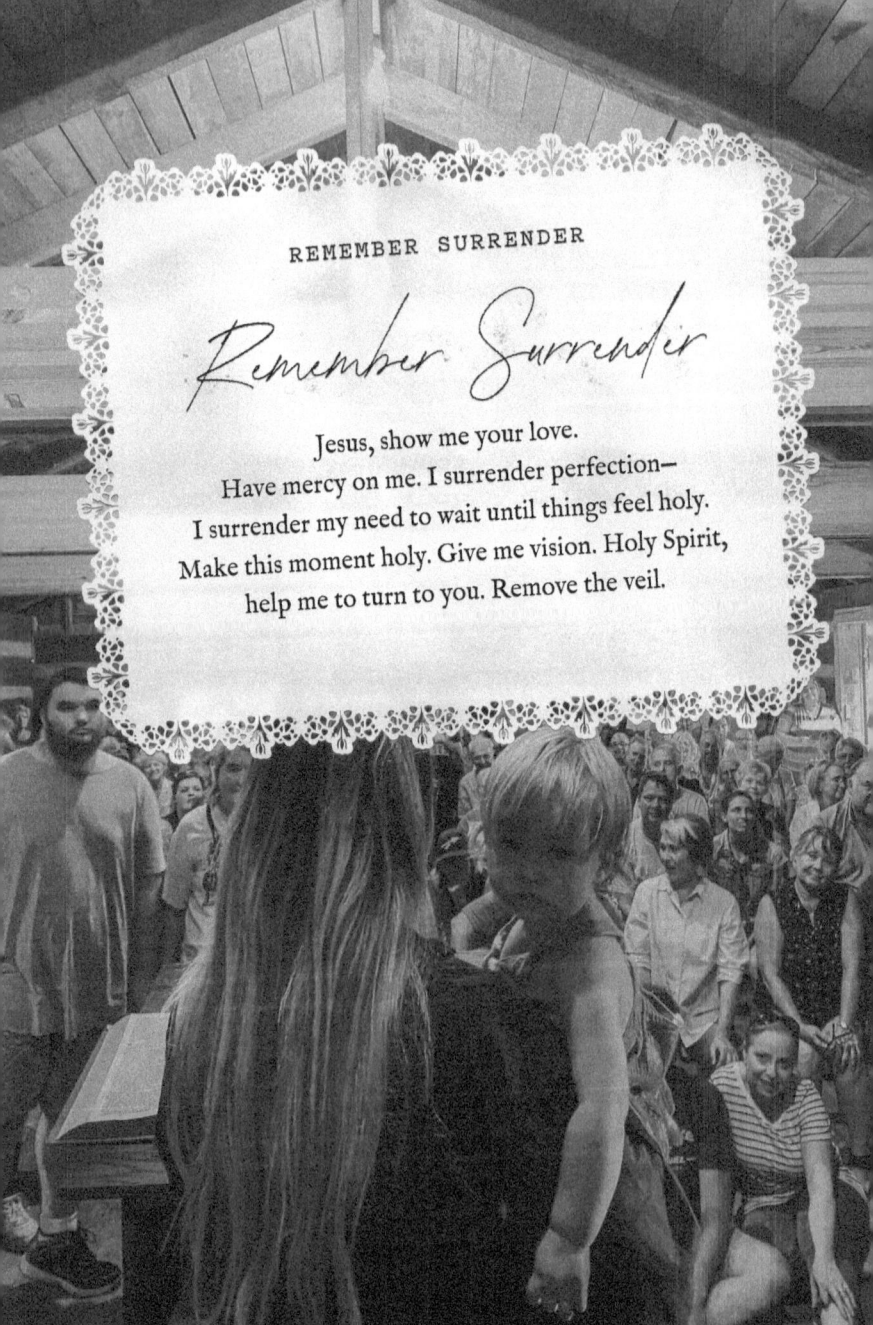

REMEMBER SURRENDER

## Remember Surrender

Jesus, show me your love.
Have mercy on me. I surrender perfection—
I surrender my need to wait until things feel holy.
Make this moment holy. Give me vision. Holy Spirit,
help me to turn to you. Remove the veil.

## Day 6: Turn to the Lord

**Remember Surrender:**

Jesus,
show me your love.

Have mercy on me.

I surrender perfection—
I surrender my need
to wait until things feel holy.

Make this moment holy.
Give me vision.

Holy Spirit, help me to turn to you.
Remove the veil.

The Presence and
anointing will
always cost you
something

Jessi Green

# Day 7
# Centering on Jesus: The Journey of Tangible Love

There are moments when the glory of God feels thick, when the anointing is tangible, and when His love feels like liquid fire pouring through every part of your being. And then there are ordinary days, when you must abide in Christ by faith. The noise of the world grows louder—and there, the real formation begins.

I used to think I could run on the anointing alone: the thrill of revival, the miracles, the power. But I've learned that without integration, without the quiet place of love, it all begins to crack. The invitation of Jesus is not merely to do His works, but to *become like Him.* And that becoming requires stillness, learning how to truly love the Lord, receive His love, and give it away to real people in real life.

Providence is my new favorite word, one Eddie gave our family. **It describes how God quietly arranges the pieces of your life when you aren't clever enough to see the whole story.** It's the idea that there is a steady, unseen hand of God guiding events, weaving chaos into coherence.

A closed door can feel like rejection, only for you to later realize it was protection you didn't have the foresight to request. Providence is not about chance; it's about trust. Every season, whether it feels like expansion or pruning, is the Father's orchestration of love. He is weaving your story with divine intention.

There are days He will baptize you with power, and there are days He will invite you to clean your house with excellence and remember the Kingdom ability within you to restore and make things better than you found them.

### Day 7: Centering on Jesus: The Journey of Tangible Love

In every rhythm—
power, suffering, silence
—He remains the same.

The Father's love is not found only in the big moments, but also in weakness. I've found that His love meets me most profoundly in the moments I feel left out, forgotten, or small. It's in those places that His voice whispers, *You have nothing to prove.*

And it's here that I learn to integrate—to let the contemplative meet the active, to hold the anointing and the ache, to gather love like treasures found every day.

> **It's burning the candle <u>now</u>,
> not waiting for later.**

When the confetti of revival settles, this is what it's all about. If I'm honest, I'm on this journey with you. I don't have it all figured out, but I'm desperate to learn. This is the kind of Christianity I want—the kind that pours its heart out in the middle of an ordinary day. The kind that pours its heart out in the middle of an ordinary day.

The world is perishing for lack of the knowledge of God, and the church is famishing for want of His presence. The instant cure of most of our religious ills would be to enter His presence in spiritual experience, to become suddenly aware that we are in God and that God is in us. This would lift us out of our pitiful narrowness and cause our hearts to be enlarged. This would burn away the impurities from our lives as the bugs and fungi were burned away by the fire that dwelt in the bush.[13]

There's an invitation being whispered to you.
Now, in your stretchy pants and undone hair.
Jesus is not the God of someday.
He is the God of here.
Of now.

"Look for Christ and you will find Him. And with Him, everything else."[14]

---

13   Tozer, A. W. *The Pursuit of God*. Harrisburg, PA: Christian Publications, 1948.
14   Lewis, C. S. *Mere Christianity*. New York: Macmillan, 1952.

It's time to take out your journal and *Light a candle*

slowly answer:

Where are you tempted to live only on the *mountaintop*?

WHAT MIGHT GOD BE INVITING YOU TO INTEGRATE INTO YOUR DAILY RHYTHMS?

○ silence

○ rest

○ reflection

○ love of others

REMEMBER SURRENDER

## Remember Surrender

Jesus, center me in Your love. Teach me to live from Your presence, not just Your power. Help me recognize Your providence in every season — to find You both in the fire and in the stillness. Amen.

"There is no such thing on earth as an uninteresting subject; the only thing that can exist is an uninterested person."

– *G.K. Chesterton*

## Day 8
# What Do You Need from Jesus?

If Jesus asked you, "What do you want Me to do for you?" What would you say?

I didn't have an answer. I drove home from a women's conference in an old, used Suburban with seven girls I discipled crammed into the back. I asked them the same question, and for the first time on our six-hour drive, the car fell silent.

The book of James can be a shock to our spiritual lives. The other day, I sat by the pool and felt the Holy Spirit drawing me in to read James slowly. James 4 says,

"You desire but do not have, so you kill. You covet but you cannot get what you want, so you quarrel and fight. You do not have because you do not ask God."[15]

Aggressive language from the brother of Jesus. And yet, don't we all wrestle—even just a little—when a friend gets the free upgrade to first class while we're stuck in the back of the plane, middle seat by the bathrooms? Or when God has promised something in your life, and you watch doors of favor swing wide open for someone new in the church, while you feel overlooked, forgotten, not chosen?

What's hardest for me is when I sacrifice time and finances, pour out blood, sweat, and tears—and someone else gets the credit. Yes, that one kills me the most.

A few weeks ago, I was preaching through the Gospel of Mark at Salt Church. I was scheduled to teach on blind Bartimaeus in chapter 10. I had pages of notes on humility and desperation. But as I read verse 51 aloud, it struck me:

---

15   James 4:2

## Day 8: What Do You Need from Jesus?

"What do you want Me to do for you?" Jesus asked the blind man.

The answer feels obvious. Jesus asked a blind man what he wanted. We would assume a blind person would want to see—yet Jesus still asked the question.

He asked for vision.

How often do I find myself asking the Lord to take care of my needs, when what I really need is to see? Perhaps vision takes care of provision.

As I read the words aloud, I realized I didn't know how to answer that question for myself. What would I ask Jesus for? Am I even allowed to ask, or has self-righteousness crept in once again, convincing me that I have no needs?

Somewhere along the way, I built a small world where I followed Jesus yet still controlled most of the details of my life. I was grateful to be forgiven. I had a thriving ministry and a healthy family. I had contentment—but absolutely zero fun.

Holy zeal had become my excuse for self-denial.

Celebration felt dangerous.
Indulgent.
Unspiritual.
I felt guilty for being blessed—anyone else?

Somewhere along the way, I built a false theology around suffering. If it wasn't hard, then it wasn't holy. I believed that being broke somehow made me more spiritual.

In reality, I was terrified to grow in capacity. Maturity in Christ meant learning how to steward wealth without worshiping it—open hands to receive and open hands to give. It meant dying to my reputation and my fear of man.

A few weeks ago, we bought a new car, and I had no idea how deeply God would use it to bring me healing. It's wild what He will use to set us free.

I had just returned from my final preaching trip of the year, freshly aware of how rare and sacred this calling truly is. I have the best job in the world—being Parker's wife, a mother to four littles, a church planter and pastor, and a mentor discipling women through *Ardently* retreats and online intensives. I also travel fifteen to twenty-five times a year to preach the Gospel, baptize believers, and support local churches. It is the best work—and it is hard work. Each year, my capacity has had to grow more and more.

In April, we sold our family car to sow into the building we were restoring. It's a beautiful white church built in the early 1800s that had been turned into a flea market.

Earlier this month, I sold the Suburban, and Parker and I began praying and talking about what my next car would be. In the last five years, we have been gifted three cars (wild, right?) and have given four cars away. Vehicles have come to represent transitions for us—especially when we lived in a twenty-seven-foot trailer with three kids.

A few weeks ago, we went to a car dealership to test-drive a used GMC. When we walked into the showroom, there it was—a fully restored Toyota FJ40 in bright yellow, with a big *NOT FOR SALE* sign on it. Parker lit up. He loves Land Cruisers. We ended up building a relationship with the dealer, praying for him, and sharing our story. God's presence filled the dealership. It never gets old—God invading ordinary moments.

Long story short, two days later, we bought the FJ40.

Then I left town for tend days to minister. When I returned to Wilmington, I drove it for the first time to Salt Church. And almost immediately, I began having an identity crisis about my new car. *What will people think of me? Is this too much? I'm a mom of four—this isn't practical. Maybe we don't need a second car. And if we do, maybe it should be a cheaper one.*

During the *Ardently* retreat I was hosting, I took a walk on the beach and began to cry. Voices of accusation swirled in my head. And then I heard the Lord whisper so gently, *Let's just enjoy this together.*

## Day 8: What Do You Need from Jesus?

It's time to take out your journal and *Light a candle*

We have full access to every spiritual blessing in Christ.
This is the truth—no matter how you feel.
Access comes through *faith*.

SLOWLY ANSWER:

Where do you experience lack?

Do you believe there is still distance between you and your Father in Heaven?

What decisions are you still making based on the approval of others, resisting God's blessing?

REMEMBER SURRENDER

## Remember Surrender

Not by striving,
not by feeling,
but by faith
we step inside.

Access is granted.
Presence given.
Love unveiled.
I'm forever invited.

## Day 8: What Do You Need from Jesus?

**Remember Surrender:**

Therefore, brothers and sisters,
we have confidence—
to enter the Most Holy Place
by the blood of Jesus.

No veil remains.
No distance stands.
Every spiritual blessing
is already ours in Him.

Not by striving,
not by feeling,
but by faith
we step inside.

Access is granted.
Presence given.
Love unveiled.
I'm forever invited.

Amen.[16]

---

16   Inspired by Hebrews 10:19

♥ being a christian is about laying down our ~~lives~~ lives because we have a revelation that Jesus died for us + rose ♥ from the grave

# Day 9
# Control or Surrender?

One of my favorite evangelists of all time was formerly a plumber. His name was Smith Wigglesworth. I highly suggest reading all of his books—faith for more will rise up in you.

Over the past six months, I've listened to the audiobook of his sermons during my forty-minute drive to hot Pilates each morning. I used to complain that there was nowhere beautiful to work out within a half an hour of my home, but I decided to redeem the drive by building my faith, praying, and renewing my mind.

Wigglesworth was fond of declaring, "Only believe! All things are possible, only believe."[17]

And yet, how often do we—with anxiety creeping in—reach again for control, instead of actually living a life of faith.

We all chase control.

Every day.

I find myself trying to bend the world, my schedule, my relationships—even God Himself—to my will, then feeling frustrated with the outcomes while still wanting supernatural intervention.

Any other *List-Makers Anonymous* members out there? We plan. We micromanage. We try to anticipate outcomes and we fail to ask God if He is even in our plans. We convince ourselves that if we can just "handle it all," life will finally feel safe, manageable, good.

---

17  Attributed to Smith Wigglesworth; unable to locate verified sermon transcript.

## Day 9: Control or Surrender?

I have the chronic problem of planning my next vacation while still on the beach with my children, enjoying the last day on the sand and struggling to be present.

And yet, despite all our efforts, something in us quietly withers. It doesn't happen all at once. It's more like a gradual drift—faith fading like a bouquet of Trader Joe's flowers left too long on the counter. A gnawing emptiness settles in, a subtle sense that the life we're living isn't fully working.

We see it in our churches, too. So many programs and ministries spinning their wheels in the name of efficiency and productivity. But in the pursuit of "success," we're missing the joy of life itself.

I once attended a pastors' conference with more than three thousand leaders from across the nation. One of the keynote speakers took the stage and eloquently presented *the* answer to the question every struggling pastor wants to know—how to grow your church in today's culture—using a case study from Coca-Cola. The solution? Become more relevant. Improve your branding. Host a pickleball competition.

I cried.

I mean, literally—I got up from the third row, ran to the bathroom, and cried. This can't be it.

The problem, though, is that control feels safe. But it's actually a cage.

When I feel most alive—when the whole "Christian living" thing is actually working—it's never in the tight grip of perfectionism. It's in the adventure. The interruptions. The inconvenient pivots. The radical generosity. It's during our family's "no-plans Saturdays," when we turn our phones on airplane mode, pray, and talk about what we want to do on our day off.

John Eldredge wrote, "Many professing Christians end up living as practical agnostics. Perhaps God will come through, perhaps he won't, so I'll be hanged if I'll live as though he had to come through . . . Like a lover who's been wronged, we guard our heart against future disappointment."[18]

---

[18] Curtis, Brent, and John Eldredge. *The Sacred Romance: Drawing Closer to the Heart of God*. Nashville: Thomas Nelson, 1997.

## Day 9: Control or Surrender?

Isn't that what we do?

In our faith, we over-strategize God's promises. We plan meticulously. We clutch prophetic words and demand the timing bend to our convenience. We build quiet time schedules that become duty rather than encounter—transactions instead of communion with our Father in heaven, who loves us.

Even sex becomes routine. I've seen reels on Instagram teaching about the "duty" of sex in marriage. You guys, this is really bad. We've turned what God designed for pleasure and covenant connection into a job requirement.

This is not a minor problem. Control is quietly killing us.

It saps our creativity, numbs our passion, and makes it almost impossible to trust God—and we hardly notice because it masquerades as wisdom and responsibility.

But there is another way.
A freer, richer, more vibrant life than anything our grasping hands could build.

It's the way of surrender.

I want to invite you into a life that cultivates habits that open the heart to beauty—morning rhythms that welcome God in, not waiting for perfection, but collecting His tangible love *now*. Practices of gratitude and generosity that shift your perspective. Moments that awaken you to see and experience the real power of God throughout your week.

My friend Cody texted me this morning, in all caps:

"TEN PEOPLE GAVE THEIR LIFE TO JESUS AT UNCW LAST NIGHT!"

I want to live life like that— a life of risk and surrender that's written in *all caps*.

## Day 9: Control or Surrender?

Kathryn Kuhlman said it best: "God is not looking for golden vessels. He is not looking for silver vessels. He is looking for yielded vessels."[19]

Surrender.
That is what heaven is looking for.
The Spirit longs for yielded ones that He can fill with His presence.

This is the terrifying beauty of surrender—to be possessed by God. To lay down the careful plans and vision boards we've written for our lives and to step into the untamed current of His Spirit.

---

[19] Hinn, Benny. *Kathryn Kuhlman: Her Spiritual Legacy and Its Impact on My Life*. Nashville: Thomas Nelson, 1999.

‹ Jessi Green's notes   ⋯ Done

September 29, 2025 at 9:16 AM

**Ephesians 2:13**
But now in Christ Jesus you who once were far off have been brought near by the blood of Christ

## Day 9: Control or Surrender?

It's time to take out your journal and

*Light a candle*

pray with me:

LORD, is there any area of my life where I am still holding onto control?

*Holy Spirit*, please reveal to me my blind spots.

Write down what comes to mind:

## Calendar your dreams and plan spontaneity.

If God gave me a word, I didn't just journal it. I scheduled it. I booked the ticket. I made the phone call. I baptized people in the ocean because the Lord said, *now*.

What dreams can you put into your calendar today?


## Accept that not every day feels like a win.

I stopped being surprised when it got hard.
The war wasn't proof I missed it. It was proof I was advancing.

This also helped me discern who my real friends were, not just those using me for personal gain.
(Oyyyy!)

Write down what trials are shaping you and what you might need to let go of.

*Tear the page out! Take it with you and live this truth.*

# my *dreams*

day / month / year

- Health
- Loving God
- Loving Others
- Personally

# my *trials*

Write down what trials are shaping you and what you might need to let go of:

..................................................

..................................................

..................................................

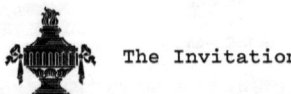 The Invitation

REMEMBER SURRENDER

*Remember Surrender*

Reject self-sufficiency.

I stopped trying to be enough.
I let the Holy Spirit interrupt my perfectly
laid plans. And I began building again from
dependence, not hustle.

**Remember Surrender:**

Reject self-sufficiency.
I stopped trying to be enough.
I let go of my staff, which was the hardest thing I ever had to do. (Cue fear of man!)
I removed myself from payroll and took a break from performing.
I let the Holy Spirit interrupt my perfectly laid plans.
And I began building again from dependence, not hustle.

Write down ways you are still relying on yourself.

## Day 10
# Fully Alive

Do you believe one question could change your life?

During the winter of 2016, while living in New York City, I had a conversation with God that changed the entire trajectory of my life.

My husband, Parker, and I had been praying and believing we would get pregnant all year. I remember looking down at the pee-soaked stick in shock, staring at the faint little plus sign in the test window. Isn't it funny how, when something good finally happens, our first instinct is to doubt it's real?

The first twelve weeks were marked by migraines, nausea, and constant vomiting. Toward the end of my first trimester, Parker and I both caught the flu. The days were long as we rolled from one couch to the other, sipping Gatorade and slowly recovering.

After the whirlwind, God met me with one question that changed my life.

It was an ordinary morning, before I had even gotten out of bed, when I heard Him ask, "Jessi, what do you look like fully alive?"

The truth is, I didn't really know—nor had I stopped long enough to ask the question. I closed my eyes and whispered, "I don't know, Lord. Please show me."

To be honest, I wasn't seeking some radical, life-altering encounter. I was just tired and hoping my "quiet time" could include a little more sleep.

As I closed my eyes, I saw myself walking along a vast beach. Then, in quick flashes, came a stream of images. I smelled the salty air and the scent of bonfires burning. I saw violent waves crashing against rocks, heard deep

## Day 10: Fully Alive

conversations about possibilities, dreams, and spiritual revelations. I watched strangers encounter God, exclaiming, "Wow, Jesus is really real!"

I saw myself preaching with passion—on piers, beneath great circus tents, and around dining room tables. In one scene, I was curled up in an all-white hotel room, overlooking the bluffs, writing and sipping tea from a delicate porcelain cup.

My soul instantly filled with hope.

But the problem was, my life at that moment looked nothing like the vision I'd just seen. I knew something had to change.

So now, I ask you this same question: What would your life look like if you were fully alive? Hear me out.

I am not asking you what your life would look like if you were a better Christian, or if you were finally recognized for your God-given talents and abilities.

I'm asking you to take a moment—a breath, a *Selah*—to pause from the busyness and constant distractions to ask the God of the universe, "Lord, what do I look like when I'm fully alive?"

I know it might seem like a strange question, but before we continue this journey of igniting revival in your heart so you experience God's tangible love daily, we must seek Him.

We throw around the word *passion* as if it were common and use it incorrectly all the time. We say things like, "I'm passionate about cooking," or "Follow your passions." But passion far exceeds excitement.

They had to create this word to describe the suffering of Christ on the cross. What Jesus endured—His physical, emotional, and spiritual agony—was fueled by holy desire. He longed for us to be free from sin and reunited with His Father. The word passion was created to describe our Savior's sacrifice, and it should also describe how we yield our lives to Him.

How, then, have we been deceived into believing our lives should be marked by dullness or indifference? How have we become so muted that we wake up, go to work,

## Day 10: Fully Alive

prepare a few meals, and fall asleep—only to repeat the same routine again and again?

It's time to stop and look at your life.
Have you grown apathetic?

Your calling is often tied to what you are passionate about—not what merely excites you, but what you are willing to *suffer* for until it comes to pass. Revival is no easy task; it is not for the faint of heart. I have wanted to quit 1,893 times this year. Yet my heart has not grown cold. Lonely, I've cried out, "God, why does it seem like no one cares? My hand is on the plow, and I can't watch one more person post about revival who won't show up to pray for it!"

If your heart has drifted into apathy, it's time to realign yourself with the One who creates life.

"For our God is a consuming fire."[20]

What areas have not yet been surrendered?

---

20    Hebrews 12:29

you now

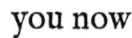 you *fully alive*

# Day 10: Fully Alive

It's time to take out your journal and

*Light a candle*

slowly answer:

Take a moment. Get alone with God.

Ask Him what He has for you -- here and now.

Write down what you look like *fully alive*.

## Day 10: Fully Alive

**Remember Surrender:**

What are three steps you can take this week to begin living fully alive?

1.

2.

3.

"But my sin was this, that I looked for pleasure, beauty, and truth not in God, —but in myself and his other creatures."

— *St. Augustine, Confessions*

# Day 11
# Behold and Transform

There's a sacred invitation hidden in the word *behold*.

It's more than looking.
It's searching out what God is revealing with wonder and expectation. In a world of constant movement, Jesus asks us to stop long enough to notice Him.

Distraction is one of the great enemies of intimacy. The clamor of our phones, the stream of opinions, even the good work we do *for* God—these can all crowd out the still, small voice that continually whispers, *I am here.* I've established a simple discipline: my phone stays in a small wooden box until 8 or 9 a.m., creating space to listen before the day begins. For months, I would feel the temptation to "research" something I was reading in my Bible, only to realize that thirty minutes later I was down a rabbit hole on social media.

To behold God is to awaken to His nearness. You cannot earn God's presence, but you can certainly make it a priority and learn to recognize when God is moving.

That's why the disciplines of silence, solitude, meditation, Sabbath, and contemplative prayer are vital. They are not religious obligations, but sacred rhythms that cultivate awareness. Holy pauses. I believe it is essential for believers to practice the spiritual disciplines and express their love for God through passionate risk-taking obedience.

**Silence and solitude** are the threshold into the life you say you want. They invite us to bypass the noise, so our souls can breathe again. When Jesus slipped away to lonely places, He wasn't escaping responsibility. He was realigning His heart. In silence, we remember who we are and who He is.

## Day 11: Behold and Transform

**Meditation** anchors that awareness. It's not emptying the mind but filling it—with truth. When we meditate on Scripture, we slow down so His Word can take root. We ask the Holy Spirit to teach us His Word and to increase revelation throughout the day. Sometimes I'll linger on a single line from the Psalms, repeating it until I reach that "aha" moment when meaning opens and understanding settles in.

**Sabbath** is where trust in your calling and purpose grows. It's not merely resting *from* work; it's resting *with* God. It's creating margin to enjoy Him, to savor beauty, to play, to invite friends over for a game night (we are addicted to Monopoly Deal). Of all the disciplines, Sabbath is the hardest one for me to keep and practice. With a busy ministry schedule, we have had to readjust which day works best for our family. Make a plan and tinker with it until you have a rhythm.

**Contemplative Prayer** is new for me. Sometimes that means sitting quietly, breathing slowly, and whispering His name. Other times, it's waiting in His love until peace begins to rise out of the day-to-day chaos. The goal isn't to "feel" something, but to "become" someone. Someone rooted, still, and deeply aware of God's presence. Eddie's favorite prayer is, "Jesus, Son of David, have mercy on me," and our family now whispers it throughout the day.

In all of this, the goal is not striving, but attention. You will fail at stillness. You will drift. You will check your phone halfway through prayer. Yet the miracle remains: Jesus will still be there.

"You have nothing to prove."
Those were the words that set me free.

Free from manufacturing energy.
Free from measuring worth by performance.
Free from trying to validate a calling I already carried.

When God whispered those words, I was leading a church, overseeing a revival ministry, and running a business. I was busy doing everything *for* Him but missing the invitation to simply *be* with Him.

Revival doesn't happen because you prove yourself faithful. It happens because you finally believe He is.

## Day 11: Behold and Transform

As we began gathering for Sunday night prayer, something shifted. Families started encountering God. Hearts came alive again. And then, almost unbelievably, a forty-two-acre farm was paid for. Debt-free. Not by striving, but by resting in His presence.

This is success in the Kingdom: not what you build for God, but what He births through your surrender.

**It's time to take out your journal, light a candle, and slowly write down:**

"One thing have I asked of the Lord, that will I seek after: that I may dwell in the house of the Lord all the days of my life, to behold the beauty of the Lord and to inquire in his temple." [21]

"Unless a person is born again, he cannot see the kingdom of God." [22]

---

[21] Psalm 27:4 RSV
[22] John 3:3 AMP

## Day 11: Behold and Transform

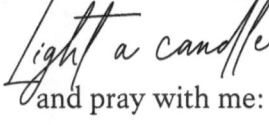
## Light a candle
### and pray with me:

Jesus, awaken me from
spiritual sleep.
Shake the dust from weary
places within.

I don't want to drift through
my days half alive,
counting breaths rather than
living with purpose.

Call me out of survival and
into surrender. Let your
light pierce the fog of
distraction, Your voice
cut through the noise of
routine.

Breathe on my soul until
desire burns again.
Teach my heart to
wonder, to notice,
to behold.

I don't want to survive
—I want to live fully
alive in You.

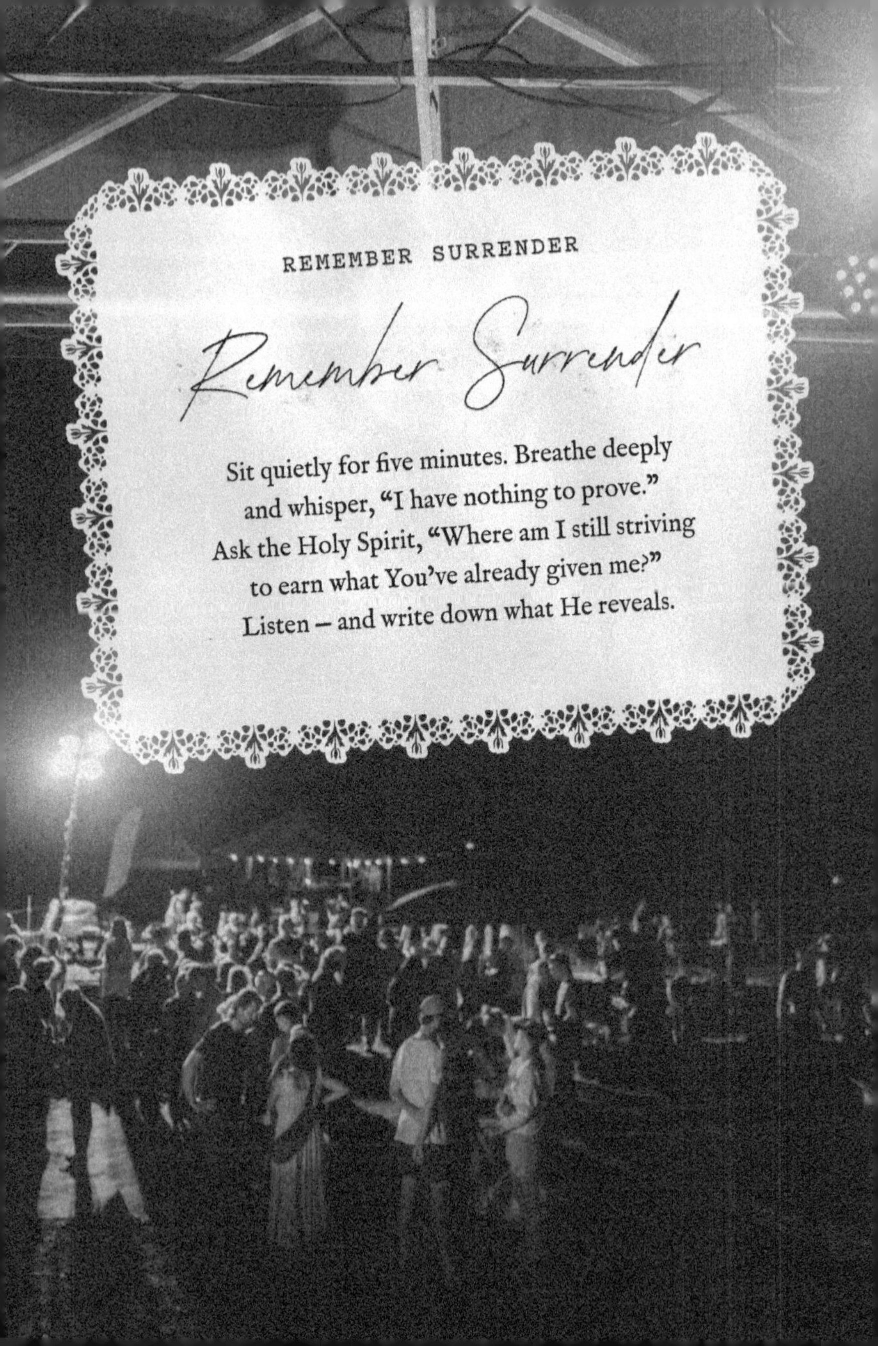

REMEMBER SURRENDER

*Remember Surrender*

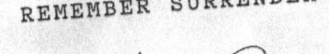

Sit quietly for five minutes. Breathe deeply and whisper, "I have nothing to prove." Ask the Holy Spirit, "Where am I still striving to earn what You've already given me?" Listen – and write down what He reveals.

*Day Twelve*

# North Star

Parker and I have a simple practice we call *Finding Your North Star*.

It's our way of pausing to ask: Where are we headed and what is all this unto?

One verse that always grounds me is Ephesians 2:10, "For we are God's handiwork, created in Christ Jesus to do good works, which God prepared in advance for us to do."[23]

---

23   Ephesians 2:10

When you are born again, a new adventure begins—discovering what you were created for. You uncover this as you spend time in God's presence, in the Word, through prophetic words, and by being rooted in a local church. God desires for you to know your purpose because it brings glory to the Father.

You may already know what your *North Star* is or you may discover it along the way. When you figure it out, write it down!

For example, at the age of eight, my husband knew he would one day pastor a church. Parker grew up loving the Word and had a passion to teach it to others. At eighteen, he went to Bible college and has been in ministry ever since.

Perhaps your path may look more like mine—a journey of discovery. Personally, my *North Star* often looks less like a single assignment and more like the kind of person God has asked me to become. Over the years, I've noticed the "assignment" changes. Some seasons have led me into the marketplace and entrepreneurship; others into full-time ministry, preaching, and writing. In

## Day 12: North Star

my current season it looks more like discipling women, creating an atmosphere of God's presence in our home for my husband and children, and leading a local church.

Personally, my *North Star* is that I am called to be a revivalist, to invite people into a deeper encounter with God's tangible love and presence. I am desperate for people to truly know that Jesus is real and that His love transforms lives.

The way my calling unfolds continues to change as I live surrendered. I'm not married to a specific assignment, but I do know who I am and what I am called to do, and that never changes.

A *North Star* helps me clarify my values, discern where to save and invest my finances, and determine how to spend my time.

One of the oldest lies is that what you do with your body doesn't matter. It began in the early church with Gnosticism—the belief that spirit is holy but matter is dirty, and that belief matters more than how you live.

It sounds ancient, but it's everywhere now.

After I had our daughter, Summer, I stopped working out and taking care of my body. I distinctly remember being in Kentucky—baptizing hundreds of people while battling a migraine, inflammation, and exhaustion. Parker looked at me and gently reminded me, "You need to take care of your body to run in your calling."

Revival exposes the lie that following Jesus is merely intellectual. When real fire falls, it doesn't just touch your thoughts or emotions—it consumes your whole self. You kneel. You weep. You lift your hands. You go. You move. You obey.

Revival always invokes a physical response.

When Jesus rose from the dead, He didn't return as a ghost or a metaphor. He came back in a body. He ate. He walked. He embraced. He breathed.

To follow Him means to live in your body as if He still dwells there—because He does.

Your hands are for healing.
Your mouth is for declaring truth.
Your feet are for carrying good news.

Day 12: North Star

I pray this *North Star* process helps guide you in the weeks ahead. You can always return to it, revisiting and refining it as you grow.

Light a candle and slowly read Ephesians 2. Let each word sink deeply into your body, soul, and spirit.

## Remember Surrender:

Have you asked the Lord, "What have you prepared for me to do?"

Is there still anything you're holding onto from a past season?

The following page is a great place to jot down some ideas. Take a pencil and write the vision down. It will be fun to see the progress when you return to it later.

*Tear the page out! Take it with you and live this truth.*

# North Star

What I believe I am called to do:

........................................................................................

........................................................................................

........................................................................................

↓ ↓ ↓

Vision one        Vision two        Vision three

↓ ↓ ↓

A Few Next Steps    A Few Next Steps    A Few Next Steps

- ○
- ○
- ○
- ○
- ○

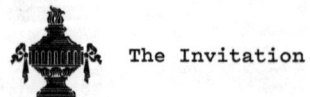

The Invitation

# Ephesians 2:4-7

*we need to understand and experience His love first*

*4 But [a] God, being rich in mercy, because of the great love with which he loved us, 5 even when we were dead in our trespasses, made us alive together with Christ—by grace you have been saved— 6 and raised us up with him and seated us with him in the heavenly places in Christ Jesus, 7 so that in the coming ages he might show the immeasurable riches of his grace in kindness toward us in Christ Jesus.*

!!!

*before we believed, we are dead in sin.*
*Are you still living dead in sin or alive in Christ?*

*do you actually believe this is true?*
*what difference would this make in your life?*
*THIS IS HARD TO BELIEVE*

"Your life as a Christian should make non believers question their disbelief in God."

— *Dietrich Bonhoeffer*

# Day 13
# Collecting Love

It was late autumn, and I booked a house with several friends to attend a four-day conference. When we arrived, I gasped. This was not a house but an estate—built in the late 1800s and recently renovated. It sat on 40-acres of land, lined with holly trees and large oaks. Stillness blanketed the property, and my heart surged with excitement.

We quickly parked our cars, and the girls and I ran into the house while the husbands trailed behind us with our luggage. We definitely overpacked, but that's a battle for another season.

As we entered through the kitchen, the house seemed to wrap around itself. Hidden rooms were tucked away, waiting to be discovered. One large, extravagant space I immediately dubbed the "flower room" featured oversized floral couches with perfectly matching floral curtains. Light poured through the expansive windows, and brass hardware gleamed on the French doors.

My friends Vic and Crystal plopped down onto the plush floral couches, and we laughed at the beauty and chaos of the room. As we wandered through the house, we found ornate crystal chandeliers, Tiffany-blue bathroom sinks, and eclectic wallpaper adorning the sitting rooms.

I woke up early the next morning to read my Bible and dig into a book before the first conference session. I was reading Colossians, lingering over the verses I was wrestling with, when God whispered: "Put down your Bible, grab your phone, put it on airplane mode, and go take pictures of everything that makes you feel love."

I threw on an oversized hoodie and began walking around the house. I played some Mumford & Sons on Spotify and took a photo of the chandelier. Then I found

## Day 13: Collecting Love

my friend Hannah sitting in a windowsill reading and snapped another photo. I approached the French doors and heard a quiet whisper, *Come outside.*

It was raining, and I was barefoot, but I decided to say "yes."

I walked around the house in the rain—my cold feet sinking into damp leaves on the rain-darkened pavement. I came across an old stone fountain and stopped. I closed my eyes as each raindrop washed over my face, and I began to cry as I felt God's overwhelming love for me.

I came back into the house and made myself a latte (we're the kind of people who bring an espresso machine on trips), and sat down at the dining room table with thirty-two photos on my phone, collecting love.

There's a reason the mystics and contemplatives could live with undiluted peace in a noisy world: they learned to absorb love in the silence. They collected the moments when the Father's affection brushed against their hearts and let those moments shape them.

For me, most days look like slow mornings with my journal and a sugar-free vanilla latte—watching light pour across the pages of my old Bible as love settles into my soul. It looks like making cookies with my kids as egg yolks splatter across the counter, or long walks with Parker around our neighborhood followed by a slow breakfast at Drift Café. It looks like choosing to connect with the people right in front of me.

These are my thin places—the spaces where heaven and earth meet in real life.

I think of it like tending a garden. Every time I read something that awakens my heart—Henri Nouwen, Charles Finney, A.W. Tozer—it's like watering a seed. Every conversation that reminds me I'm loved adds sunlight. Every tear shed in prayer softens the soil.

The spiritual life isn't about chasing the next encounter; it's about cultivating an integrated rhythm where divine love infuses ordinary moments. Contemplation becomes the undercurrent of our doing.

## Day 13: Collecting Love

We can't live on the Mount of Transfiguration forever—Jesus didn't. He went down into the valley to love, to heal, to suffer, to serve. That's where the journey continues.

So maybe the invitation for us is this: to collect love wherever it comes, to nurture it, and to let it form us into people who reflect Jesus to the world.

## Day 13: Collecting Love

It's time to take out your journal and

*Light a candle*

slowly answer:

**what** "thin places" in your life make you aware of the Father's love?

**who** has God placed around you to remind you of His heart?

**how** can you make small, consistent investments in your own soul health this week?

**Remember Surrender:**

Father,
teach me to collect love in every season—
to see You
in faces,
in silence,
in laughter,
and in tears.

Help me build a life
that integrates Your love
into every part of who I am.

Let my soul be a garden
where Your presence
grows deep roots.

Amen.
Now take fifteen minutes
to walk through your home,
photographing everything that
awakens love in you.

REMEMBER SURRENDER

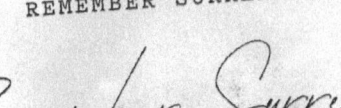

Help me build a life
that integrates Your love
into every part of who I am.

Let my soul be a garden
where Your presence
grows deep roots.

# THE INVITATION

## Day 14
# The Gift of Faith

Faith isn't just a feeling—it's a gift, a posture, a choice to trust God even when the road ahead is unclear. It's what allows ordinary people to live extraordinary, supernatural lives. Faith opens the door for God to move in ways we could never orchestrate on our own.

But faith doesn't grow in isolation; it grows in surrender. To believe is to release control, to step off the ledge of self-reliance and place your trust fully in the One who is always faithful.

One of the most powerful ways to cultivate this gift is through confession. Confession isn't meant to punish us; it's meant to free us. When we bring sin and weakness into the light, shame loses its hold. Confession positions the heart to trust God's mercy, reminding us that He is for us, not against us.

As you confess, breathe deeply.
Let the weight fall away.
You can trust Him with every area you've tried to manage alone.

Faith begins where self-sufficiency ends.

Worship is another gateway to faith. When we lift our voices in praise, we proclaim truth over our circumstances. Worship turns our eyes away from what we see—lack, fear, confusion—and toward what is true. God is good. God is powerful. God is near. Even in moments of uncertainty, faith grows as we declare His faithfulness aloud, rooting it in our hearts. Worship is faith in action; it is believing before we see.

Surrendered prayer leads faith deeper. Like Jesus in Gethsemane, we learn to pray, "Not my will, but Yours be done." Surrendered prayer isn't passive; it's trust in motion. It lifts our desires, fears, and dreams before

## Day 14: The Gift of Faith

God—and then lets go. It releases our grip on outcomes and settles us into the confidence that God's purposes are perfect. This kind of prayer aligns our hearts with His, allowing His faith to flow through us.

Lectio Divina—the ancient rhythm of reading Scripture slowly and prayerfully—teaches us to wait on the Word. Instead of rushing to form a conclusion, we pause, meditate, and listen. We allow a single verse, a single phrase, to move from the mind into the heart. We begin with a simple question, "Lord, what are You saying to me?" and then wait for His gentle whisper. In the stillness, faith takes root, quieting our need to reason our way forward.

Faith is not a performance; it's a gift.
Surrender is not weakness; it's strength.
Together, they invite us into a life that is alive with hope, freedom, and the supernatural power of God.

Today, believe.
Release control.
Confess.
Worship.

Pray without borders.
Listen to His Word.
And step into your calling with the quiet confidence that He is faithful.
The gift of faith isn't earned. It's received when we stop gripping control and start trusting Him completely.
Surrender, now.

Surrender is not abstract. It is lived out on ordinary Tuesday afternoons—and in hospital rooms, when suffering comes knocking without warning.

Every morning, I light the wood-fragrance Buck Mason candle beside my bed as I hold my baby, Madison. I choose to remember: I have nothing to prove and nothing to earn.

Kathryn Kuhlman once preached, "I surrendered unto Him all there was of me: everything! Then, for the first time, I realized what it meant to have real power."[24]

That is the secret, friends.
Not striving.

---

24  Kuhlman, Kathryn. *Nothing Is Impossible with God*. Englewood Cliffs, NJ: Prentice-Hall, 1964.

## Day 14: The Gift of Faith

Not grasping.
Not controlling.
Not fame, status, or riches.

But burning.
Yielding.
Surrendering.

This is how we revolt against the illusion of control—not by trying harder, but by opening our hearts wider to the invitation to trust.

"Now faith is the assurance of things hoped for, the conviction of things not seen."[25]

"For by grace you have been saved through faith. And this is not your own doing; it is the gift of God."[26]

What is the gift of faith? Faith is not positive thinking. It's not emotional hype or mental toughness. Faith is the supernatural ability to see Heaven while standing on earth, born from abiding in God's presence.

---

25  Hebrews 11:1 ESV
26  Ephesians 2:8 ESV

In Greek, *pistis* means to be "persuaded by God." When the Holy Spirit gives you the gift of faith, you begin to live with the conviction that what He said is more real than what you see.

Ephesians reminds us that faith itself is a gift. It cannot be earned—but it can be cultivated. As we spend time in His presence, in His Word, and among people full of faith, our belief expands. Obedience becomes easier because trust has taken root.

Do we all have faith? Yes. But the gift of faith goes deeper—it is the Spirit placing His own confidence within us, empowering us to break through unbelief.

Faith is contagious in proximity. When a community steps into it together, faith multiplies and the supernatural becomes normal. Trusting God in the unseen trains our eyes to recognize His Kingdom everywhere. Some live immersed in it while others only brush against it, because faith is risky love—it says yes before the guarantee. Miracles, provision, and transformation are not rewards for "special people," but fruit borne by those who believed God meant what He said.

Day 14: The Gift of Faith

Today, make a commitment to go all in. Lay everything down at His feet.

EPHESIANS REMINDS US:

faith itself is a gift.

OBEDIENCE BECOMES EASIER BECAUSE TRUST HAS TAKEN ROOT.

REMEMBER SURRENDER

*Remember Surrender*

Go find a leader in your church and ask what it would look like for you to go deeper in your relationship with Jesus and serve the local body.

# The Invitation Lifestyle

There is a moment when the noise finally quiets—when striving, performing, and proving fade into the background—and you realize that the only thing that ever truly mattered was abiding.

Revival doesn't begin with movement; it begins with His presence. It begins with union in Christ.

I remember standing on the beaches of Huntington, drenched in salt water and tears, watching people rush into the Pacific Ocean to be baptized. It was holy chaos—men and women dying to themselves and coming alive again. Yet beneath the roar of the waves and the shouts of worship, the Lord whispered, *Follow Me, not momentum.*

Abiding is not passive. It is deliberately choosing stillness in a world addicted to acceleration. It is refusing to let your fruit outpace your intimacy. This was the hardest lesson for me to learn.

The wildfires of revival are not sustained by zeal alone; they are sustained by those who remain in Him. Jesus did not ask us to perform *for* Him—He invited us to dwell *in* Him.

When I think about that summer of revival, I don't only see the baptisms or the miracles. I see faces. Men and women who discovered that Jesus was not merely real; He was near.

That is the secret to sustaining fire: abiding love.

Because fire untethered from intimacy will always burn out.

It's time to take out your journal and

*Light a candle*

slowly read & answer:

"Abide in Me, and I in you. As the branch cannot bear fruit of itself unless it abides in the vine, neither can you, unless you abide in Me."
John 15:4

WHAT THREE THINGS STAND OUT TO YOU?

one: ............................................................................................

............................................................................................

two: ............................................................................................

............................................................................................

three: ............................................................................................

............................................................................................

**Pray with me:**

Jesus,
teach me how to abide in Your presence.
I don't want to perform for love,
I want to live from it.

Settle my heart
in the quiet knowing
that I already have access.
Your nearness is not earned—
it's given.

When I forget,
remind me again
that belonging is my beginning,
not my reward.

*Amen.*

## Remember Surrender:

Sit in stillness with no music, no performance, no pretense. Breathe deeply and whisper, "I am here, Lord. Teach me to remain."

In the quiet, recognize that abiding is not about doing more for God, but about being fully present with Him. There, love steadies your soul, and His presence becomes the place you live, not a place you visit.

Ask the Lord, "As I live in your presence, what does it look like to transform the world around me?"

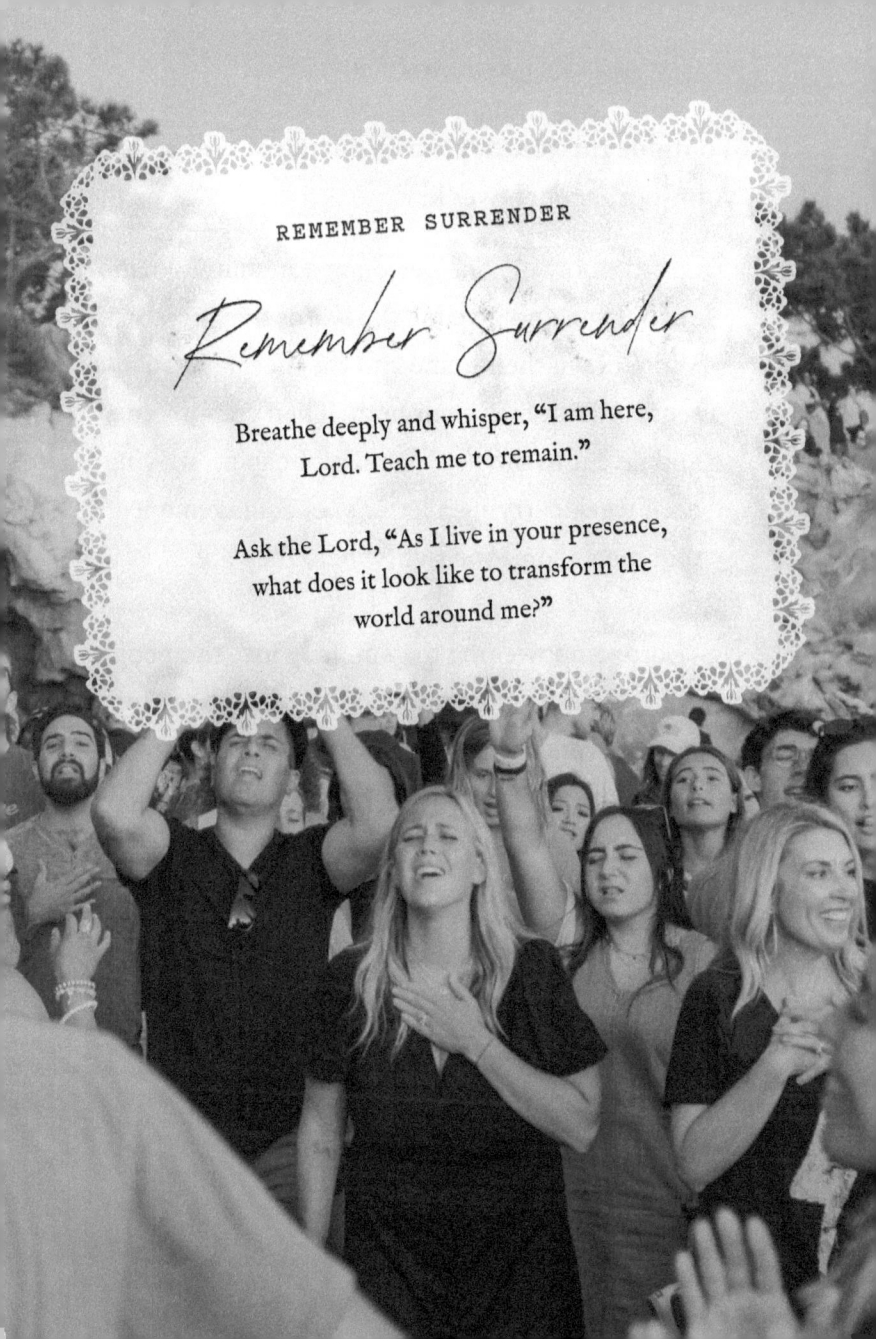

## REMEMBER SURRENDER

### Remember Surrender

Breathe deeply and whisper, "I am here, Lord. Teach me to remain."

Ask the Lord, "As I live in your presence, what does it look like to transform the world around me?"

**To continue this journey, write down your responses in your journal each week:**

1. "Lord, show me one person in our church I can encourage, and give me the words they need." Write down their name and the message you sense will awaken their faith. Then craft a letter and give it to them on Sunday. Imagine arriving each week carrying a letter of encouragement that meets someone right where they are.

2. "Lord, empower me to genuinely love the people around me. Highlight one person I can pray for in public and share Your love with. Help me overcome fear." Each day, record the person you prayed for and the moment you shared the gospel. (If this feels stretching, you can join my *Soul Winners* course at jessi-green.com.)

3.  "Lord, who in my life needs this devotional? Show me who to bless and invite to walk with me. Teach me how to make disciples." Freely received, freely given.

4.  "Lord, I lay every gift, passion, and dream at the feet of Jesus. Every resource, every dollar, every possession belongs to You. How would You have me steward all that You have entrusted to me?"

# Pause

Before you turn the final page, slow down. Let the words you've read settle into your bones. Notice where your heart softened, where resistance surfaced, where hope quietly reawakened. *The Invitation* was never meant to be consumed—it was meant to be received. Mark what has shifted. Name what is still unfolding. Transformation rarely arrives with spectacle; more often, it takes root quietly in good soil. Trust the work that has begun, and keep walking with Him.

| DAY | COMPLETED DATE | REVISITED |
|-----|----------------|-----------|
| 01  |                |           |
| 02  |                |           |
| 03  |                |           |
| 04  |                |           |
| 05  |                |           |
| 06  |                |           |
| 07  |                |           |
| 08  |                |           |
| 09  |                |           |
| 10  |                |           |
| 11  |                |           |
| 12  |                |           |
| 13  |                |           |
| 14  |                |           |

# About the Author

*Jessi Green* is a revivalist and preacher who helps believers live fully alive in Christ. After a radical encounter with Jesus in her Manhattan apartment, in 2009 she sold everything and traveled the nations as a missionary, hungry to find the "real Jesus."

Jessi resides near the beach in North Carolina with her husband Parker and four children David, Ethan, Summer and Madison. She is the director of Saturate Global; a grassroots revival movement that is uniting the church to preach the Gospel and baptize thousands. Alongside her husband, Parker, she also co-leads Salt Church in Hampstead, teaching and equipping the church in hosting the presence of God, winning the lost, and making disciples.

Jessi believes that Jesus came to give us life and life more abundantly.

You can follow her on Instagram
https://instagram.com/jessi.green

Or online at Jessi-Green.com

# the Ardently intensive

*A month of pressing pause on distraction and saying yes to Presence, yes to vision, yes to faith. In community, with daily Scripture, Spirit-led formation, and live sessions, you'll be sharpened, stretched, and set on fire. This is your invitation to prepare the message God has placed in you, to see with heaven's perspective, and to live ardently—fully alive, fully surrendered, with hearts on fire.*

jessi-green.com

*Ardently*

## SIMPLE STEPS TO GET INTO
# God's Presence

JESSI GREEN

SIMPLE STEPS TO GET INTO GOD'S PRESENCE

## burn a candle

create a place that is set aside
where you expect Him to meet you

JESSI GREEN

> ✓ Read books to that teach you what He is like and how to be in the Secret Place, use a journal to write down what sticks out to you or what you hear Him saying. Set a time and pick a place to meet with God everyday

**JESSI GREEN**

# Wake Up Early

| | | |
|---|---|---|
| 8 P | put kids to bed | 7:30 – 8:30pm |
| 9 P | nighttime routine | 8:30 – 9:30pm |
| 10 P | bed | 9:30 – 10:30pm |

✓ Go to bed early so that you can wake up early. Make spending time in His Presence a *priority*

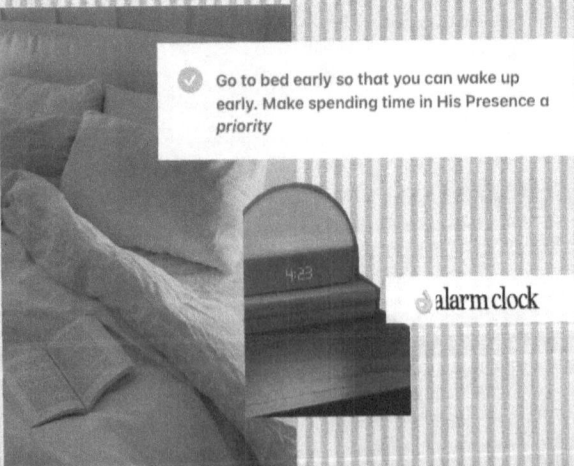

alarm clock

# SALT CHURCH

## We exist to worship Jesus, to know Him and to do what He did.

A church in Wilmington, NC

Salt Church is a nondenominational church led by Parker and Jessi Green. A church full of God's Glory, where every member of the body of Christ is alive and actively participating with the gifts God has given them. A church at war against the gates of hell that sets the captives free, heals the sick, and raises the dead as we continue the commission of Jesus.

www.saltchurches.com · @saltchurches

Additional Activation pages have been
included for you to complete.

Tear these out!

Embrace this call to apply what you've
read and learned.

It's time to take out your journal and

*Light a candle*

slowly read Psalm 91:1-16

"Whoever dwells in the shelter of the Most High
    will rest in the shadow of the Almighty.
I will say of the Lord,
    "He is my refuge and my fortress,
    my God, in whom I trust."

Surely he will save you
    from the fowler's snare
    and from the deadly pestilence.
He will cover you with his feathers,
    and under his wings you will find refuge;
    his faithfulness will be your shield and
    rampart.
You will not fear the terror of night,
    nor the arrow that flies by day,
    nor the pestilence that stalks in the darkness,
    nor the plague that destroys at midday.

A thousand may fall at your side,
    ten thousand at your right hand,
    but it will not come near you.
You will only observe with your eyes
    and see the punishment of the wicked.

If you say, "The Lord is my refuge,"
    and you make the Most High your dwelling,
    no harm will overtake you,
    no disaster will come near your tent.
For he will command his angels concerning you
    to guard you in all your ways;
    they will lift you up in their hands,
    so that you will not strike your foot
    against a stone.
You will tread on the lion and the cobra; you
    will trample the great lion and the serpent.

"Because he loves me," says the Lord,
    "I will rescue him;
    I will protect him, for he acknowledges
    my name.
He will call on me, and I will answer him;
    I will be with him in trouble,
    I will deliver him and honor him.
With long life I will satisfy him and show him
    my salvation."

The Invitation

**JESSI GREEN**
—— WITH LOVE, ALWAYS

# my when/then lie

When:
..................................................................................

Then:
..................................................................................

When:
..................................................................................

Then:
..................................................................................

step two - copy the statement

*Now! I choose to follow Jesus now.*

↓

BEHOLD WHAT HAPPENS.

Notice the peace that rushes in when you
stop delaying surrender.

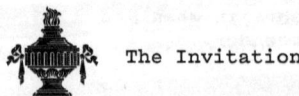The Invitation

# my when/then lie

When: ..................................................................................

Then: ..................................................................................

When: ..................................................................................

Then: ..................................................................................

step two – copy the statement

*Now! I choose to follow Jesus now.*

↓

BEHOLD WHAT HAPPENS.

Notice the peace that rushes in when you
stop delaying surrender.

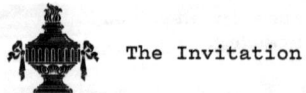

The Invitation

## my *dreams*

day / month / year

- Health
- Loving God
- Loving Others
- Personally

## my *trials*

Write down what trials are shaping you and what you might need to let go of:

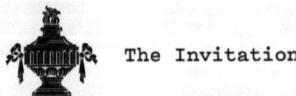 The Invitation

# my *dreams*

day / month / year

- Health
- Loving God
- Loving Others
- Personally

# my *trials*

Write down what trials are shaping you and what you might need to let go of:

..........................................................

..........................................................

..........................................................

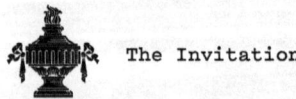 The Invitation

 JESSI GREEN
—— WITH LOVE, ALWAYS

# North Star

What I believe I am called to do:

..........................................................................................

..........................................................................................

..........................................................................................

↓ ↓ ↓

Vision one       Vision two       Vision three

↓ ↓ ↓

A Few Next Steps     A Few Next Steps     A Few Next Steps

............ ○     ............ ○     ............ ○
............ ○     ............ ○     ............ ○
............ ○     ............ ○     ............ ○
............ ○     ............ ○     ............ ○
............ ○     ............ ○     ............ ○

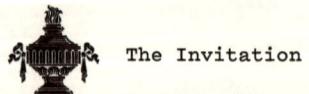 The Invitation

# North Star

What I believe I am called to do:

.................................................................................................

.................................................................................................

.................................................................................................

↓ ↓ ↓

Vision one          Vision two          Vision three

↓ ↓ ↓

A Few Next Steps    A Few Next Steps    A Few Next Steps

- ..................... ○
- ..................... ○
- ..................... ○
- ..................... ○
- ..................... ○

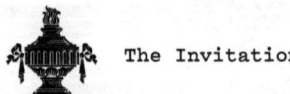 The Invitation